AEONIAN ZEPHYRS

RASHMI SHUKLA

To the seekers of meaning in every fleeting moment,
To those who wander through the labyrinth of life, searching for truth and beauty,
This book is for you.
For those who believe in the magic of the—the "more" that exists between words,
In the spaces where dreams meet reality, where silence holds its own verses.
May these poems guide you towards discovering the understanding of endless possibilities of
life, love, and imagination.

With AEONIAN ZEPHYRS one travels:-
Whispers of eternal winds, timeless and free,
Carrying dreams across an endless sea.
Boundless and gentle, they caress the soul,
Guiding us softly toward an unseen goal.

Contents

Contents

Preface

AEONIAN ZEPHYRS is a narrative poem/poetry/letters book composed by Saiyaahi Inks aka Ms Rashmi Shukla that spins tales through verses blending her experiences with the rhythmic beauty of poetry.

Each poem captures moments, characters, and emotions, unfolding like chapters in a novel. The rhythm and rhyme guide will progress the readers through epic adventures, intimate dramas, or effectual memoirs.

The language is kept rich yet concise, using imagery and metaphor to evoke deep emotions.

Themes often explore human nature,

love, loss, and fearlessness, with a focus on distinctive experiences.

The poems are structured yet fluid, offering a unique fusion of literature and poetry that appeals to both the heart and mind.

Acknowledgements

Creating this book has been both a personal and collective journey, a weaving of emotions, thoughts, and experiences into verse. I stand on the shoulders of many who have made this possible.

To my late parents Mr.Chandra Shekhar Shukla and Mrs.Kalawati Shukla, who nurtured my love for language and expression ,also for their continuous guidance in life for rectifying my mistakes . I thank them for giving me the freedom to explore my creative passions. Their love and belief in me has been the foundation of everything I do and will do all my life.

They still continue to be my strength.

To my husband Mr.Rajib Choubey who have had always been my best critic in my writing journey.

I'm also grateful to my siblings who kept pushing me towards accepting challenges with an optimistic approach.

Also I'm thankful to my friends, colleagues who offered feedback, encouragement, and the occasional nudge to keep going, their support has been invaluable. They have been sounding boards giving inspirations in my creative journey.

To my mentors and fellow poets, thank you for showing me that poetry is not just a form of expression but a way of life. Your guidance has enriched my understanding of what it means to write with purpose and depth.

To the readers who have picked up AEONIAN ZEPHYRS, whether by chance or choice—thank you for allowing these words into your lives. I hope these poems resonate with you, provoke thought, and stir the depths of your soul. Without your willingness to explore the unknown, this book would be incomplete.

And lastly, to the essence of poetry itself: the unseen force that binds us to our emotions and to each other. Through poetry, we understand the world in ways words often fail to explain, and for that, I am eternally grateful.

Thank you for embarking on this journey with me. Let us continue to search for the —the "more" that exists within us all.

ACKNOWLEDGEMENTS

Thank you
Rashmi Shukla

1. MISTAKES

'Ever thought why our lives are always so confused and naive,
In spite of trying all the tricks, we miss to flow with speed in the wave.
To understand what's right or wrong, mind becomes nothing but a slave,
No matter how hard we try, a weak moment comes and takes to grave.

Mistakes are such woes that we don't want to ever happen,
But destiny pushes our instincts unintentionally it misshapen.
In that very instance moving ahead seems to be a great decision,
but eventually, beauty of that learning sinks to lose its precision.

Not being prepared for life's extremes was my biggest mistake,
Life's become so critical, it never allowed me to prepare for any retake.
Dealing with it, makes me feel like residing near the dried cascade,
still! I did had the hopes that one fine day it will definitely serenade.

I crumbled and failed but had the courage for learning every day,
It was not easy to gather strength when all your closed ones just ran away.
Uhh! It showed me light as high time to systematically manage life anyway,
Hiding faces is never a great solution for errors ,come what may.

Yes! Now I'm in a better position to handle my family in any crisis,
To move on is life, regretting for long won't change willpower's chases.
A stumble here, a wrong turn there is bound to take one miles,
Through trials faced and paths not straight will only enhance lifestyles.

Life's not perfect nor am 'I', I take just a step at a time to synthesize.
Let people say whatever they want to, they exist just to capitalize.
Accepted!! That making mistakes in any weird situation is humane,
Life will always be like a roller coaster ride and not a smooth plane.

2. MY TEACHER, MY HERO
(Angel In Disguise)

I was the colour which my teacher painted bright,
One who gave life to my thoughts & brought ideas to light.
In the life, full of ups and downs I made many mistakes,
My teacher showed me the correct path at every single stage.

Silly things attract more and we tend to go along,
He helped to realize the difference between right or wrong.
True, I had to work hard and reach my goal all alone,
Where and how to start right, my teacher had shown.

My Teacher showed a new and brighter vision of life,
Whenever I was lost in darkness and lost hope in strife.
The one who mapped to explore the world on my own,
Motivated me to walk the untraveled paths all alone.

My Guru clapped, and shared my achievements with pride,
In spite of his scolding ,encouraged to do better at every stride.
His style of being happy was to say-DON'T HASTLY FLY, KEEP A CHECK,
I was truly inspired by him, to never bow down my neck.

This was the key mantra by which I could see some success,
He was my second parent, who moulded my life not any less.
Teachers are our heroes, who are truly Angels in Disguise.
My teacher was my hero, who took every effort to make me wise.

THANK YOU FOR BEING THERE SIR

3. ACCEPTANCE

Move around to the soul, you've rejected the other way,
bring back your deep glazing touch, and don't leave this way.
Leave not my darling, as you had left at no convey,
The shattering pieces of identity, that's gone with yesterday,

In the stillness of the dark consuming night,
Whispers of the past takes a rapid flight.
Wounds and scars from beyond limits the softly fade,
In the peace convincing reality that we have made.

Storms that once severely raged now gently rest,
In the intriguing generous heart, a quiet quest.
To accept every tiny fact only to forgive,
In the light of bafflement, we choose to live.

Shadows linger phenomenon, but don't stay,
Morning is sunny and chirpy, brings a brand new day.
With each breath ensuring life, a chance to be,
Free from chains of drowning thoughts, completely free.

Passionate consideration for you may be wondering,
May not have been understood more or less quarrelling,
Respect and have Acceptance of every sage,
Forget what's happened and live in large every age.

4. TILL I DIE

Don't leave me till I die,
Don't ever let me cry.
I want to be as fresh as a flower,
Don't ever let me dry.

Shower me with love
don't let me feel low.
I want to burn like a candle,
Don't ever let me blow.

Don't ever be apart,
Don't let your love depart,
I want to be with you forever,
Don't ever break my little heart.

Don't ever let me detach,
For tears like rain never catch,
Where joy and warmth in hearts abide.
In laughter's light let us reside,

With every smile, we heal and grow,
And let our emotions flow.
So hold me close and dry my eyes,
Together we'll chase away the skies.

Don't ever tell me a lie,

Don't ever let me sigh,
I want us to be together,
So never say good goodbye ever.
Don't leave me till I die......
Don't ever let me cry.......

5. SECRETS TO STRENGTHS

We often see across many kinds of unique relationships,
People are deliberate to be happy in their companionship.
So instinctive to make the real work of commitment,
although, sometimes it shows effortless temperament.

Ignore the silly quarrels, do not drag the reason endlessly,
Landing up in the beginning of a beautiful World optimistically.
We often see across many couples showing conscious care,
they are keen to unite, this quality displayed is so rare.

These souls are happy to accept the responsibilities,
proud do they feel, to convert their amicabilities.
These instances are lived without any compulsions voluntarily,
Secrets to strength is to work with the connect invariably.

We often come across many lovey doves observing loyalty,
by being empathetically drawn they never blame destiny.
Reconciliation is always in the mind and the heart store,
they want to grow together in extremes even more.

Resilience blooms in courage of silent flights,
Strength is born with every breath in the darkest nights.
They are always blessed with abundant well wishes,
Minimising down desires and expectations wishes.

6. WANDERING HEART IN PIECES

If you remember the way we looked,
at each other or you just forgot conveniently.

How are you going to look in my eyes?
When all the time you are obsessed with lies.

Do you ever feel the craze to walk with me?
Its real wandering heart in pieces surrounds now just me,

It's really sad you are making up for stories,
When all my pieces of heart know the truth series.

Every time I spent time you made me feel better,
However, too much involvement mutually got changed later.

You wandered with my pieces of heart broken,
Tears inconsolable ,how I thought you were my chosen?

A wandering heart bleeding in pieces torn,
By love once bright, now left scattered in forlorn.

Fragments scatter lost in pain eventually with time,
Echoes tearing us apart with a distant chime.

Yet in the shards iridescent, hope still gleams,
A path to mend gloriously, through tender dreams.

This abstract miserable feeling of your ditch disgusts,
Can't even imagine to do what your heart adjusts.

I continued with reality to get every fear soaked,
What was the reason of this ruthless act made heart choked?

I had lost my heart for you to hold life and shower care,
But my blind trust left me broken-hearted nothing to share.

Like two estranged souls we wander with broken-heart pieces,
You kept lying and lead life with lies with no eases.

Now let's be fair and give extreme space to each other, no teases,
let's set an example so there's no more wandering heart pieces.

7. SOCIAL BURDEN

Please make me understand......
When we deal with daily complexities,
Why can't we choose at times to breathe in relief?
When we deal with unwanted cuss to categorize simplicities,
Why the problems creep at intervals and life's not dealt with belief?

Please make me understand.....
When we always try to give people around our best,
Why this so called society keeps light bird's eye view?
When we are ready to alternate unclear the feasible test,
Our guilt and instinct sways like pendulum to hold on to the review!!

Please make me understand....
Why is it to be forced from ages to follow a set of norms,
We are those lives who are blessed to live only for once,
And wander to manage the challenges we face in different forms,
Already keeps us on toes to manage with dignity and life's trance.

Please make me understand....
Why is it expected to appease a Social burden,
The same society neither allows nor forgives error,
No! Take life's lead and deal ups and downs in passion,
Unless we deal diplomatically how we will live happily forever.

Please make me understand.....
When society take charges required to live,

We need to indulge existence to give society its due.
Calm down when haul hits insanely for shades of cool hive,
Believe to check mate this freight and smile along with the best hue.

8. ESSENCE OF LOVE

Love is beyond definitions, creates an everlasting bond,
swaying away in your beloved arms, and is of what I'm fond.

Essence of love is embodied ever within my partner's fragrance,
Feel him passionately all over in ecstatic mood's salience.

In the moments to touch extreme intimacy, we're glued,
Skin to skin, breathe to breathe holding in sync understood.

Charisma of this embrace is so beautiful, we want it forever,
This night is already making plans to serenade us together.

Love's essence lies in tender grace, a gentle touch, and a warm embrace.
In whispered words and gazing eyes. Where silent bonds, like stars arise.

It's in the moments of soft and true . Where hearts unite, forever new.
Love's essence in a touch so kind, a whispered secret, hearts entwined.

In silent glances, warmth conveyed, through every moment, love displayed.
A bond that's pure, a flame that stays, lighting our hearts though all our days.

Indeed all wish to live and breathe this choice in reality,
we're fortunate to find eternity anytime in soul's sanctity.

9. PEOPLE BLAME

Trace the road we are trudging up to the hill,
Agreed that mistakes bounty happens with no will.
When every movement of yours is scrutinised,
convenient way for people is to blame being characterised.

Especially when its Woman, the blame game intensifies,
The reason be it social or personal, its 'SHE' who sacrifices,
No one has time to even ask what she truly testifies,
And we just pity again to censure why do you'll so sighs.

People blame baselessly and cast their stones,
Forgetting sins today from past within their own.
In shadows deep, tall and black their judgements lie,
While truth witnessing and grace pass swiftly by.

People blame without hearts of struggles,
Forgetting faults within their instinct juggles.
Their words can wound, their eyes can pry,
Yet truth and kindness existing today never die.

Social norms are drastically queer with twists and turns,
High time we understand and have empathasize to earns,
Blame game will always fetch one a broken family and society,
Stop blaming!! Forgiving is the need of the hour to shower morality.

10. RED MOON

People live life differently, yeah!! On their own terms,
Ocean of emotions push at right as our mind churns.
Instances from past keeps on toes and tearing us apart,
The more we try to control, from within the revolt starts.

Plethora of feelings wiggles deep within the oh! Heart,
the sign of our love, the Moon is too turning smart.
Though it looks bloody and creates immense impact,
why, at times feels like breathing is totally hijacked?

In spite of knowing things will never be the same again,
Wish the ones we loved for them to accumulate the gain.
This night is comprised with a stiff RED MOON story,
Except for the part of tears washed through a mystery.

The Aura has become passive with boggling intensity,
Mind is not ready to accept this denial of density.
Hold on! When the situation like this often aligns,
Positivity of our existence glitters & morning shines.

11. AN UNSAID GOODBYE

Lovely were the days when we were together,
Life was beautiful when heart was willing to surrender.
Time bends all the rules for ever being happy 'Craters',
the closed ones are forced to convert as strangers.

Relationship becomes so complicated at times,
be in it or move out off, kill instincts and break spines.
The aura itself tears you apart for going so far,
that's the need of the hour, and breathing can't be at par.

No point in being along when it suffocates,
Distancing oneself from the moment percolates.
Time will make to suffer as one and deny acceptability,
Wounds given by the most loved one kills the nobility.

An unsaid goodbye insanely lingers in the air,
A silent sorrow, burning with a heavy despair.
In quiet moments, revelations in memories rise,
Echoes of laughter in pace with unspoken goodbyes.

"An Unsaid Goodbye" makes you feel useless,
Sun shines in front but that respect and warmth collapses.
Years passes by and all the efforts goes in vain,
And one starts living with never healing pain.

12. MY PERSONAL QUEST

"I am grateful for being alive
to discover my quest,
Day by day, month by month
to sync in with the life' zest.

Who am I? What for I'm here,
What's the purpose of my birth,
Desperately trying to recognise
and minimise the mind's dearth.

The art to learn and practice
of meeting self every day,
Self-consciousness plays an
immense role at the every bay.

Moments of self-fulfilment
creates juggling peace,
I struggle, I fall and then to stay
strong at chance's ease.

People come and go from life
with very purpose to challenge,
Giving up can't be any kind of
a solution even if you scavenge.

Not a single prediction helps

ever, to sustain in scarcity,
Self believe to sail out in any
adversities just brings proximity.

Every day will be a new day,
Take it as it comes to sustain,
Being sure of myself will only
help the pain and struggles doesn't pertain.

My personal quest will keep
reinstating with conscious time around,
To live, to smile, to adopt and to share is
that's what is life all about.

13. NOTHING IS IMPOSSIBLE

When I step out in the arena of
acute and intensified darkness,
little do I know one forward foot
might take me to the World's madness.

I dream, I strive to the hilt many
a times failing to almost the core,
I break into pieces like morale is
falling in a pit, draining all the more.

Life doesn't end there, I wait,
I try to the best of my purest capacity,
"Nothing is impossible", this belief
Has to be practiced with maximum intensity.

Gather yourself and mend shattered pieces
For it is you, who need your kind self,
Start from where you stand in the moment
Endless waiting for an opportunity has no life shelve.

Vibes of positive reflection carry you miles
and overcome ones negativities,
Take control of the situation,

For it is you who will explore the possibilities.

Determination will always be the key
to give you kick and sleepless nights,
Being Crazy as they may call but will
certainly push you to achieve wishes rights.

Be it even the "Black Hole", every
question has an answer in this universe mapping 'zen',
everything damn' is possible only thing is to
Ensure that "YES I'LL MAKE IT HAPPEN".

Eliminate all the impossible elements
and gather the altering perspective,
Flush out the defeatist attitude and attempt,
Engage with sheer perseverance indeed subjective."

And yes of course the famous saying goes
"IF YOU CANT FIND A WAY, CREATE ONE"
Truly Believe this.

14. POWER OF BLESSING

"She is an Urn...
In a palatial corner,
And her thirst is not watered
Rare pious ones,
will be able to quench the draught drying...

She is a book...
Placed in a dusty woody shelf
and her cover is the climax
a bibliophile
will be able to grasp the expressions flowing.....

She is a wind chime....
In a cul-de-sac
and her skin is a melody
Very few men
will have the pleasure of hearing....

She is a prayer....
Echoing at a dead end
and her verse is the silence
The ones spiritual
Will have the power of this blessing.....

She is a quilt
Folded along the lap

and its feel fabric is the warmth
Very special ones
will have the feel of the contended wrapping.......

15. CONSCIENCE

"Every person's identity is shaped distinctive to the core,
Characterised on their upbringing true all the more.

Self-expression of thoughts and ideas sets one apart,
Digging mind to the last layer of knowledge fills cart.

Taste and style upgrades with evergreen moulding style,
Brightens anyone's dullness when they see you Smile.

A little memory flashes and make you see through self,
Interrogate many a times about existence of worth shelve.

Like no one, not even a single one, will be to similarity,
Conscience keeps displaying your character with clarity.

The way one manages crisis, in any phase of life,
Shows one's personality to the World as a different strife.

Adapting to the situation is what makes you to bear fate,
Sensitivity is what makes one humane and refrain to hate.

Trust, honesty and being practical, empathetically is bang on.
While dealing difficulties, with ease and life keeps going on.

16. UNDERSTANDING AND MISUNDERSTANDING

*Paradox of life swings like a pendulum between psychology and reality.
Right from one's birth we jiggle between our thoughts, perception, history,
memories, experiences and related surroundings till date.*

*Our mind's box is filled with unlimited emotions and unexplainable waves that
sometimes breaks you and many a time's gives hope to take it easy and move
beyond.*
*These involves narrations of one's understanding that is totally unfounded
and unexplainable at times.*

*Eventually, these actions and reactions with whom we are emotionally or for that
matter even professionally connected , their stuff matters as they acts as agents to
our opinion directly or indirectly.*

*And then yeah.....our lives moves between understanding and over understanding
of such situations.*
We humans are extremely sensitive beings and get hurt........
*Sometimes we want the whole World to know about it and sometimes go into our
shell in silent space of the "ME" zone.*
*We understand situations and transactions based on our thoughts and how we
want to see it. And let me tell you in life it's not always about black or white, at
times its grey too.*
*It's very rare that we put ourselves in other person's shoes to have an understanding
from his eyes, from his view.*

We just keep blaming others that they don't understand us.
Have we have ever intrigued, a big no!!
Yup! In spite of claiming that we are selfless, it's then where we become self-centred
and self-conscious.
Then begins the series of misunderstandings about the person or be it situations.
Lack of communication and time constraint aggravates the already bad situation
to worse.
We need to understand, that everyone has their own mind-set and they behave
accordingly. So for even them, we need to empathetically behaving.

Space and distance, indeed plays a massive role in absorbing the shock and
understanding things in a much better way.
Never ever out life's graph will be going up. It will have abrupt jerks, unexpected
twists and turns with absolutely no idea what to do when with whom!
Who will befriend, who will console will always be like a mystery taking one closer
or farther from extremely close ones.

It's our problem, we need to deal both ups and downs related to them.
Least expectation will help us sail through any discrepancies or confusions.
If we are understood.....fine and even if we are not, then let time deal with it.
For whom we matter, will stand with you with every thick and thin without
critically analysing you.

Let me conclude:-
"Forgive and have your peace of mind,
Be accommodative and let time be kind.

17. COMPANIONSHIP

"Life was never the same......
since the time we first met,
It was like a dream come true,
Ultimately I got you as my
soul mate without any regret.

The sweet nothings.....
That we have been sharing along
Your happiness and contentment,
Is all that I wished and prayed for life long.

Ups and downs of many kinds.......
Trespassed our companionship many a times,
Since love is not only about sharing highs ,
Lows in life that we managed, now beautifully chimes.
To understand and let go off....
I took my feet back as I wanted you to lead
these decisions weren't taken in haste
rather these resoluteness didn't let us anyone plead.

Many instances brought.......
alternatives that grovelled us to dilemma,
Patience and trust in you
Gave me the KICKASS attitude to make our vibes Aurelia.

You mean the World to me......

Truth of life far away from fantasy,
Conscious efforts I took along
to do my every bit and make your likes the reality.

Oh! My Darling!!My partner for life.....
I will always opt for being your shadow
to stand along shoulder to shoulder
and till eternity absorb all your sorrow.

Never will I bring the question of who?
Between "YOU" and "ME",
By God's grace this will surely
make us reach together the destiny of "WE".
My love for you will always be for you......
And Nothing's going to change my Voice,
Between my choices and your choices,
I chose our choice."
Yes!!My Love
between my choices and your choices,
It will always be about "our" choice."

18. LEISURE

"After a long time, today
I went for a late night drive,
So busy were the schedules,
life was just a mere strive.
Anxiety was at peak and
wanted to hold on to breathe,
Days were passing by in
the hush bush shiny wreath.

Why there is no time to
wait and look to reassess,
All of us are just running
blindly to match that space.
We are so engrossed to
forego what's happening around,
high time to take backseat
and let ease make you surround.

Its ok to prove the right
purpose of coming to World,
But to what extent will we
stretch ourselves curled.
Self-introspection is one
thing we need to do regularly,
Irrespective of what people
feel we need to move slowly.

One life multiple purpose,
some achieved some lost,
Sometimes being in zero ,
checks realised not to be tossed.
Do fulfil all your responsibilities
with flare without stare,
Take out time for leisure
to the core & rejuvenate.

Late night drives kicks
me to the core and rejuvenates,
To be wrong or doing
nothing is humane before gate.
Value Self-worth and stop
being one's life's wrecker.
Taking drives acts as my
stress medicine, I feel better.

19. FALLING OUT OF LOVE WITH YOU

"My love for you was
the only reason to survive,
Your carelessness
has brought this bitter truth alive.

The endless wait for you
Went absolutely in vain,
I lost my soul's identity
To fetch true love in life's gain.

Though our love was sweet
Too much of it caused bitterness,
Blaming each other at small faults
Hyped the let go-off differences.

Our love will always be in
Protected in good memories,
But due to the complications
It might suffer till centuries.

We tried to reconcile at any cost
But efforts went futile for sure,
Living together is next to impossible
Falling out of love with you all the more.

• 31 •

20. LIFE BETWEEN THE PAGES

"My innermost feelings came
alive on this surface,
Time, place and topic ruled the
matter with such ace.
A look taken around made my
thoughts extremely vacant,
That was the time when I
scribbled being impatient.

Let me confirm the medium
as the single source of energy,
Indeed the only witness that made
happy and sad synergy.
Moments and preferred instances were inked,
Had it not been that piece of paper ,
as my burst bag I would've sinned.

Life's was never to breathe in,
with several complications,
Be it any emotions ,the pages
absorbed these allegations.
At times I broke and the other
times gathered myself for compilations.
Certainly, it worked like a true

layer of hopeful protection.

My palate was always pouring
of ideas and emotions,
Not all the time it was bout
penning but also reading notions.
"Life between pages" was about
realistically feeling the unfelt,
Inch by inch the episodes of
fantasy too were beautifully dealt."

The reviews and differences
didn't matter to me at all,
The "ME" time with sips of
coffee took me to another World's fall.
These pages are nothing less than
my peace of mind relieving from cages,
It won't be much if I call
it as "LIFELINE" breathing in pages!!

21. MONSOON EVENINGS

In deed the wait was over!! After bearing the scorching heat for months, June had arrived. The days highly awaited by the crop growers as well as the ever thirsty ones. The first showers were here to cool down the intensity of life's disturbed paths and inconsequential burden.

The season which makes everyone just refreshed to fill life with romance and liveliness. Be it any age brings memories to galore. Sometimes sad, sometimes the most beautiful ones. Walking down the lane last night while returning from office.

Mumbai, city of Rains, the time was in 90's when I had been here with Mummy Papa. Had joined new company for new assignment.
I remember the incident so afresh in mind.
Had to stay back for board conference the next day till around 9:00PM at night.

I kicked my Kinetic Honda in the heavy showers but in the parking, the scooter was almost was submerged and water had reached the petrol tank. Those were not the days of Ola/Uber unlike today. Neither the local trains were running as tracks were filled with the flow. Phone's network were put down totally. The city had come to a standstill in the heaviest rainfall recorded that year.

Yes, it was Dadar Station I remember .Office was 2Kms away and somehow almost swimming in the road water reached the platform where trains were still. People said this is the only option and way to reach. Let's pray that level of water gets down the track to make it run.

There were few other Women who were sitting in the local. Some fisherwomen were also there with their harvest to sell in the wholesale market. I was just glaring here and there and praying for the run to start. After sometime started feeling hungry, had nothing to eat.

That was the time when the other females offered me some Ginger Tea so that I feel warm within. The station vendors fried Samosas and started distributing at around midnight to all the passengers waiting in hunger. It was like that night the classic example of the fact that still today humanity is left in this World. Some people are still there who help selflessly.

It was unbelievable that night that these are the gem because of their noble deeds. That day no one was left hungry and the sight of the fact, some people still make faces happier. At around 4AM in morning, the trains made people reach the destination.

The monsoon evening in those moments brought an all together a different World were people make the World a better place to live in.

That Monsoon memory is carved so fresh till today in my nostalgic space!!

22. ACE PHASES OF LIFE

"Ace phases of life races against
In ode to gruelling scenario,
Black is seen all around although
Wind makes difficulties glow.

Gathers the strength to diminish
Every null n negativity with hope,
Illumination shall prevail here
Is the only motto in spite of probe?

Basking in the moments to spare
The pious thoughts of the craving,
Can't leave in any situation to cover
The sight and constant graving.

Instances, when its lighten up
To give support, will and appreciate,
It melts till the wick dries,
To the last drop spending life to mediate.

No one is bothered to the feel the pain
It goes through invariably,
Always taken for granted,
That its life is to surrender inconsolably.

One life breathing, few hours within

RASHMI SHUKLA

The darkest nights is captured,
Yes, the make of its body is such that
Its existence will be remembered."

23. THE TRUTH BEHIND LIES

Sometimes a habit
sometimes becomes a need,
Telling lies intensely
is absolutely a situational deed,
Be it a white lie
in spite of its awfulness,
Disturbs life extremely
And has consequences.

Situation arises
when need is to save life,
With no reason
character is assessed at Knife,
Howsoever one tries
to convince the lies told,
Certainly violates
the sanctity of the moments at hold.

Told for betterment of
loved ones without harming,
Creates scars if intentionally
done at wounds swarming.
The impact of which
ruins someone's rest of the lives,

Goodwill created such
that destroys ones image still alive.

The base of these lies
can never take one longer,
With time and destiny will
find its face sooner or later.
Although if it shakes confidence
Its required to be said at times,
As for a minute hope brings
life to almost people dead at times.

Speaking lies which
often every human makes,
Such life is rare when
truth and its sanctity to reveal it takes.
The only thing that can keep
a check with what intention it is said,
To create or destroy the moment
Is its capacity that's always unsaid.

"The truth behind the lies"
will always have to be explored,
Before reacting and scattering the reality
Will always take one's mind-set to mould.
Like truth, lies will also be
an inseparable part of everyone's existence,
To understand the reality, it needs persistence.!!"

24. INTENTIONS PLIGHT

"The truth was unveiled
when our life comes to stake,
Crisis causing situations
leads too many a times be fake.

It actually doesn't matter
what's your side of the story,
With no time in hand
Everyone is in hurry for glory.

Life throws you to instances
Filled with utmost unpredictability,
Twists and turns in minutes
Shakes the foundation in stability.

Whom to prove right,
who'll certify one's intention's plight,
All has own versions of the fact
Conclusions depending on the sight.

Going to what level states
that judging is the easiest ever,
Empathy is absconding as efforts
for the goodwill is acknowledged never.

Hustle bustle of ones lives

pounces the need for being at peace,
the greed of power snatches
the feelings and emotions with ease.

The ability of accepting failure and
moving ahead is the need of the hourly ties,
hurting no one purposely kicks life
where the only saviour is just embracing lies.

25. EMOTIONAL MYSTERY

"Destiny brought us together
to unlock an emotional mystery,
Unimaginable feeling started
growing rarely found in any History.

Locked in your arms
I found myself secured,
Scattered outburst calmed down,
The way love was passionately poured.

Your warm hugs and sweet smiles
Brightens my day with a strong belief,
Call it my luck or the future way ahead
My mind, soul, body in you found relief.

Small efforts taken to be with me
Strengthens my confidence to set free,
I cannot bear to pull away
When towards your face I see.

I race to see you day and night
Live mere your presence around,
N' when you look into my eyes
I fall for you all over again in no bound."

26. A LETTER EXPERIENCED!!

10th Jan' 2023

Dear Sweeties,

"We were just kids when we fell in love." yeah!! This is what my gloomy memories now can talk about my first love and hello…… hahahhaa!! I can't believe you 'all are actually inquisitive to know about my love story, kidos.

Isn't it a bit strange?? A grandmother sharing with her grandkids about those lovey dovey days.

Nevertheless, listen to few of those instance that still stands afresh and brings smile on my wrinkled face.
Aaaah!! It was the real growing up days but in fact we were too young to even understand about our likings and choices. The only thing we wanted from life was just to be together and do everything together.

We were in the same school and staying in the same locality. All games to be played in afternoon after returning from school. Since our class division we could meet only during recess time in school as he was two years senior to me.
But commuting by the same auto rickshaw helped to talk minds during dawn and then dusk.

Playing and swinging together in the society garden was the best evenings spent

during childhood.
Kids, we were so engrossed that unless we talk for hours we won't eat food.

Neither our parents knew nor we ourselves that we had an extremely special connection and in spite of the future assignments taking us apart, we will be brought together by the faith in destiny to become soul mates.

We went for higher studies to two different cities and made focus to excel and fulfil parents' wishes and we did that too. But never got romantically involved with anyone rather continued missing each other. His father also had got transferred to another city for his banking job so even the family connection was lost.

Those were the days when there was no social media working or for that matter even mobiles for communicating.
You won't believe kids during those days' people use to wait for Sundays to talk at subsidized rates that too after 11:00PM with loved ones from the PCO booths!! There were no landlines also at every home.

Post studies after joining the internship he came to my city from various sources and it was only after realising post so many years that we had to be together and then we convinced family for their willingness to go ahead.
We loved each other to the moon and back and continued to live happily with extreme togetherness and great companionship.

So in a nutshell, I would like to just reiterate a point that the whole universe works on the decisions of destiny and we act according to its plan. In spite of the story that started in childhood, despite that we didn't even what love means from anyone outside family, we could share and spent life when the right time came.

I'm self-astonished that I could say what I had to and now it's your turn to choose and act wisely and value your relationship!!

Stay blessed all!!

With loads of love n best wishes!!
Your Nanny!

27. IF MY HEART WAS A HOME…...

"If my heart was a home....
it'll surely beam with positivity,
Filled with every corner will be hope,
While eradicating guilt n' negativity.

The rooms in my heart
will encircle sensitivity and empathy,
Criticizers will be thrown out for sure
Life is about showing gratitude in legacy.

The Sun peeping in from veranda,
will warm up and radiate the sunshine,
The pillars holding the walls and beam
Will strengthen even failures not to decline.

The hanging chandeliers
Will brighten every effort to love thyself,
Responsibilities will be fulfilled
Time, space, opportunity in pace to forgive myself.

Soothing and cool colours on walls
will bring in the broken pieces together
the sighs and smiles will
have to synchronise in life forever.

Due respect will be given as
Every relationship has to be valued,
Forgiveness as a virtue to practice
On the lounges, love and happiness will be glued.

28. MY FAVOURITE PLACE (Goa ....Still Unexplored)

To the King of sand ,castles, Churches and beaches pristine,
Party begins from Sunsets and continues till the Sun shines.
Enriched with the light moments, Serenity and on the rocks wine,
We begin our voyage and quickly try to catch the train before time.

Stations of Thivim, Madgaon, Karmali and Vasco are passing sway,
And the route will take us to the destination where we are going to stay,
Casinos, night life, happy faces bindaas attitude with no grudges plays,
Adventure and exploration of mesmerising jubilant Goa begins today.

Heading towards the beautiful day off we go with on friends on the vroom,
8 bikes and 16 people decked up putting on the fluorescent beach costume.
To follow the condition that no one will ever touch phones and chat rooms,
That was the place of relaxing, distressing and relishing natural beauty to its tune.

The entire city has stunning beauty, green forest and its own historical saga,
Life welcomes you there at Beach Anjuna, Amarante, Calangute and Baga,
Cool breeze at shores with beautiful sunshine keeps kissing our face,
That's where we realised life has indeed no worries in this space.

Always hurry to get soaked in sand and rush at the shore opening shoe lace,
We chased the layers of waves one after the other excitingly to shine in face,
When we be there never ever felt like coming back to return on the wheels seat,
All the time sand just covered our attitude, moods and wishes top to feet.

In spite of visiting 10 times, Goa.....Still is all the more unexplored is always a treat,

Goa is not just one beach city but actually an emotion from soul to feel mystic.

The Goa Carnival is a lifetime experience which everyone feels to tweet,

Goa will always be my favourite years after years feel proud to be part of sea pleat.

29. HOPE

In life when you fall gather your strength
Failures are bound to happen in length,
Intervene instincts to avoid cannon,
Your hope will make things happen!

In life when our loved ones leave forever
One has to deal with it as strongly than ever,
Ages in life keeps moving unintentionally,
With the good memories that dies never.

When life shows darkness all around,
Talk to your soul to enlighten,
That's the right time to show courage
With hope screen negativity to brighten.

No one else will give you that hope
You are the only one who will cater oneself,
Don't surrender to situations anymore,
Wait ;analyse , try and succeed yourself.

Give yourself the best company
In successes and failures of life,
Calmness and peace only should matter,
Ultimately before leaving this World just thrive.

Gift yourself the best gift- HOPE!!

30. MY INSTINCTS

Taking the road in solitude was the option left,
I screamed , I silenced , I roared to be arrest,
Yes, arrest within my thoughts, instincts to the core,
Just wanted to be in peace and only that more.

I sought determination thereafter to live free,
I said "YES" to every opportunity in my way to agree,
Questioned myself do I really need the person,
One who broke you in pieces, why would require any permission.

In quiet whispers instincts call,
A guiding force, unseen by all.
Through twists and turns they lead the way,
In shadowed night or the brightened day.

They pull me toward the unseen light,
A beacon shining ever bright.
With trust in heart and mind so clear,
My instincts guide me, quell my fear.

Expecting the one will never help you rebuild,
No, enough is enough now , it's your need to be refilled.
"I Started loving myself when" I realised my Worth,
It's only me, who'll remove negativity from dearth.

31. LETTER TO MY FUTURE!!

Dear My Future,

Hope you now have pleasant surprises in the coming years. Time has made the days so quickly that it makes me feel half of my life is gone struggling, learning and reactivating with my experiences.

As I'm progressing towards you please maintain the strength with me to enable to manage any crisis and shocks that God has poured in my kitty.

However, also please ensure that both my mental and physical health holds the capacity to keep me calm and in peace. May you please reinstate the inner power to forgive if not forget things.

Let me know and make you remember that I see myself playing and dancing with my grandchildren with specs and wrinkles on my face happily. I want to wear smile with utmost grace whoever I meet and whenever I look into mirror. I will not mind to see myself with white hair or blurred vision.

Only thing I want you to safeguard my ability to fulfil my responsibilities with glee before I say final Good Bye. What matters to me is not a very large life but whatever number of days I breathe should be content and free of pain.

It's your wish to make it challenging or to give a smooth life decorated with rough patches. I just want you to know I practice THINK FOR THE BEST YET PREPARE FOR THE WORST,

Even during uncertainties I just want to give the best even if you fail.

Highly obliged to you
Rashmi Shukla

32. FAVOURITE CUISINE: - LITTI-CHOKHA

"Never can anyone forget
the taste of my village dish.
As I step towards that side,
my heart gives me appreciation.
Since childhood,
have savoured the delicacy in mesh,
It looks amazing all the same
even after years of association.

Be it summer holidays
or cold nights, you would understand.
When reaching crossroads
after passing through the village trails.
The fragrance that used to
make me crazy from far away stand,
Crowds used to gather every
evening, tasting in long queues in rails.

So presenting here is my favourite
"litti-chokha", the desi delicacy,
Even if it is cooked,
the taste of smoky balls will be sharp.
Cooks with brinjal, tomatoes,
chillies with round potatoes easy,

Eat it hot or stale
heart doesn't cheat with any harp.

Bring flour from roasted
gram when you go to the market,
A piece of ginger, four cloves of garlic.
Beating with hot green
chillies and chopped coriander socket,
This wonderful mixture of sattu(red gram's flour)
and pickle mixed with spicy flick.

Awesome tasty food that
takes care of health to the core,
Also its cooking doesn't use
much oil lasts for days together.
Prepared In the eastern regions
generally and savoured with heart,
There can't be any replacement
Of LITTI-CHOKHA In World Apart.!!

33. ALMIGHTY

"Without blessings of Almighty
no success is complete,
However, we try to trace our steps
Nothing can be built in concrete.

Hope, courage and right attitude
Are the answers received in prayers,
Self-confidence is boosted
In trying times with shades and layers.

Power of blessings is such
That one's decisions are encouraged
A rock-solid enigma is created
with kick ass attitude even if we are caged.

An unknown force that is Supreme
Makes darkest moments in strength display,
We will get through vehemently
Believe in God everything will be Okay.

34. WE ARE DIFFERENT PEOPLE BUT.....

"World full of mixed emotions and feelings
Right from birth to death its various dealings,
Culture ,upbringing and exposure shapes personality,
Circumstances comes to twist and turn such formality.

We are different people but ultimately peace matters,
Not always in the riches but basic living too chatters.
How so ever you keep running behind the glamour,
A day will come when everything fades at no harbour.

Some crave for position while some for power,
Recognition is never fetched with luck but hard work devour.
Happiness and health subsequently one aspires for,
Family plays the most significant role truly inspires for.

Choices and preferences never matters but smiles does,
Sensible and optimistically sensed people appreciate timeous.
Just "BE YOU" without pretending to others for the sake,
In this packaged universe, initiate to love and breathe without break.!!

35. MY CITY-JAMSHEDPUR

Whether you love it, or hate it hard,
My love for ""Jamshedpur"", cannot be barred...!!

Roads are broad, parks are green,
This is the BEST city, I have ever seen...!

By rich & poor, society is not walled,
Proud i feel when ""Jamshedpurian"" I am being called...!

The crime rate here is relatively less,
City is nicely built, not a mess...!

We call it ours, not just my,
I love the most, place called ""Jugsalai""...!

Then there are ""Bistupur"" & ""Sakchi"",
Heart of the city & commercial centre...!

Every businessman wishes to invest here,
In some or the other venture...!

Other places like ""Kadma"" & ""Sonari"" are on the other side,
Where every inhabitant of the city loves to reside...!

""Adityapur"" is known Jamshedpur's Industrial Belt,
Where all small scale industries, are duly dealt...!

The famous green & ravishing spot,
Is known as the ""Jubilee park""
Preferred place for morning walks,
And couples in the dark...!

Places like ""Dalma"" & ""Dimna"",
Are our city's proud...!
That makes us yell ""Jackpot"" is the best,
With our voices loud...!

TATA STEEL of Jamshedpur is the biggest producer of Steel,
Thousands of people depend upon it, for their daily meal...!

JAMSHED JI NUSSERWAN JI TATA,
Was founder of this place,
We celebrate his birthday on March 3ʳᵈ every year,
Decorating ""Jubilee Park"" with lights and jubilation

JAMSHEDPUR IS THE PLACE WHERE MY HEART TRULY BELONGS
TO

36. MILLION WORDS FOR MY HEALING!!

"Peeping him daily for years from the room's corner,
Getting his one look instance was such an honour.
Seeing him walking along the dense hostel lanes,
Finding excuses to watch him from the glass panes.

Thoughts entangled to let him know the feeling,
Smile he wore spoke million words for my healing.
One sided love expressions owes to silent confessions,
Longing for just one touch becomes life's possessions.

Life got surrounded just around what he projects,
Step by step , day by day search in love detects.
Dreaming day and night about spending life with him,
Profound was his presence in life for me from within.

His Aura made my World come to a sure standstill,
Frightening was mere his denials if anyhow he shares will.
Writing letters anonymously was never a good idea,
Left his willingness and acceptance for the memory galleria.

37. LOOK INTO MY EYES!!

Look into my eyes darling! To rise beyond emotions,
Hold me extremely close and seal thy relations.

To it, is for you and me to feel this pure intensity,
Drip by drip sync in to nerves and live love with velocity.

Little did I know here, what destiny was instigating,
again and again reading you is always mind boggling?

It's beyond my capacity to make you solely realise,
Meeting you at this stage, now life seems to synchronise.

Look into my eyes and see the depths of the invasive soul,
A story untold, where countless dreams unfold.

Glimmers of hope, gruelling shadows of fears,
Whispers of love listening through the fleeting years.

A universe breathing within, boundless and wide,
Where passions reside and secrets within confide.
In the quiet gaze, find the truths we disguise,
Discover the World when you look into my eyes.

Do you mind if I call you "My Man" with accord,
though never expected yet accomplished my Lord."

38. FETCHING FREEDOM

"The only thing ultimately matters is inner peace,
Come what may fit ones conscience at ease.

Let not your zing upbringing be ever be questioned,
Fetching freedom in hard work is to be only mentioned.

Overthinking will unnecessarily add on to worry some mood,
Remove all the chaos and let yourself called as shrewd.

You are unique and has to set own rules with signature style,
none can rule your dimensions, be adamant to go miles.

Fetching freedom from the chains unseen,
In the quiet moments where lonely hearts convene.

Boundaries fall eventually, the spirits rise,
In the open air beneath exists endless skies?

A journey begun, with steps so light,
Toward a horizon kissed by the dawns first light.

Fetching freedom from ever growing life's constraints,
In the breath of dawn, where the wandering spirits paints.

Breaking barriers, without guilt embracing the breeze,
Unshackled hearts with almost the unfound ease.

A dance with destiny, bold, beautiful and bright,
Liberation is often found in the softest light.

The aura around you will truly reach as higher,
Aesthetic Thoughts and deeds will make you flyer.

Create such vibes that your presence is felt in silence too,
your domain will set you apart in memory after essence too.

39. SCHOOL MEMORIES

Fascination of Red Pomp Shoes
Yeah, Those were my first ones,
Flashes say ,year was grade second,
That was Choir, where I'd to shine like Sun,

Being the third amongst four siblings,
We were taught and trained to the core,
with share in happily, every belongings
I had to listen and simply give away more.

Every single penny went in piggy bank
After every visit at grandparents place,
When summer vacation came for us,
Brought back to school that rupee solace.

Me and two more adventurous friends
Were allowed to cycle down in grade fifth,
Along the whole side roads we paddled,
And promised fulfilling friendships myth.

Rs.2 was the cost of idli chutney
That was served on Mahua leaves,
Post which we dodged Golgappes for Rs.5,
Sweet and sour tamarind were savour believes.

Enactment and mimicry of teachers,

We're the favourite pass time in their absence,
The monitors were compelled to take breaks
And we ruled with extravagant rambles in presence.

Exhibitions and flower shows
always had grand openings in Winters
With full dedication and excitement
we participated till school was in dusty splinters.

Sports day and picnics were a must,
Participation was compulsory for all round development,
Talent of every child was visible,
We realised it's importance while being transparent.
Academics and curriculum
more than kids, botheration was for parents
Exams and results were the priority
Prestige and tight collars were declarants.

Every miniscule were taught to use
Crafts and projects in group were the best,
Learnings in subtle guidance
Created, An everlasting impact ruling test.

Since I was in Catholic School
Prayers before tiffin were compulsory,
Churches in school opened on Saturday,
Kids followed the divine power for losses recovery.

The teachers coached for equality
Boys or girls!! Rustle always prevailed,
Everyone pushed themselves with hard work,

Sooner or later success witnessed was detailed.

"SCHOOL MEMORIES" are like Topsy turvy,
  Moments filled with tears in grade Tenth,
  Learnings and adventures was continuous
In heart, will always hold most special plinth."

40. THE LIFESPAN OF MISTAKES

"Life always brims with
smiles and frowns,
we take God's decisions
by stride while being his clown.

No one's perfect
so are none of the life's rules,
while proceeding towards
responsibilities there is no one right tools.

Absolutely, it's not fair
to crib over few blunders,
Take it as experiences
through which learning ponders.

Acceptability of being
A failure is a must to excel,
It's actually these mistakes
That polishes in circumstances to dwell.

World around is anywhere
Having an eagle's eye on you,
At least one should forgive self
And come out of blame game itself.

Roads that we walk
Will never we like a bed of roses,
We walk, we fall , we wait , we again get up
And understand errors molecular doses.

Uncertainties and risks
Shows Prudent and prolific lives
get over the lapse done in the past
Screams and yells be over bearing Knives.

"The Lifespan of mistakes" shouldn't
dominate and disturb all your breath,
Inner instincts and self-realisation
Should empower and help in this birth.

Never ever curse oneself
Aberrations and miscalculations no long,
It's OK to err, yet learn from it
Time changes ,so shall you get strong.

41. COLOUR OF MY HEART

"Lost in the glimpses of the
sight, I see often with wide eyes,
Few things exists for a reason,
a reason with no reason arise.

Though darkness prevails
A moment I seek for some light,
That's the only source
Giving me hope to witness the next daylight.

A layer, people wear on mind
Controlling their thoughts over me,
I chant prayers divine
God's blessings will shower upon me.

Look back and watch
the tumbling past moments
a rush of flashes crosses my veins
instantly turning blue in ailments.

Happier times undoubtedly
helps me sail through the depth,
Beats get into pink with aplomb
Far from belief ,that's my inbuilt strength.

Being in proximity to my beloved,

Emotions are red -crimson of course,
Visible spectrum of dimensions
My levels reciprocated is lifeline source.

Comfort and cosiness
I find in giving sheer happiness,
Being available in someone's need,
Orange is my feeling, cheers in brightness.

"Colour of my heart" is Contented
Just as I proceed where life takes me,
Acceptability while being agile
Is the belief imbibed in black, breaks me.

42. STORIES WE NEVER TELL

"Few incidents or instances
that's buried deep inside our mind,
Thoughts that's already flashed across
It's for the person experienced to unwind.

Moments of pain to anger
Witnessed to the core and recorded,
Lovable clichés is in mind's hanger
Looking in flashback, silence is rewarded.

It's not about ones
acceptability to speak to the World,
Few "Stories we never tell",
It's impossible to understand hence Swirled.

None other than Self Instinct
Know the purpose of tales to be quiet,
Highest level of criticism knocks
Stigma attached can't be erased to white.

Feelings and emotions
has no boundaries but is compressed
Value of those occurrences
without explaining to others shouldn't be suppressed.

43. DUSTED PAST

"Turning the pages that's by now almost torn,
an era where miniscule of my dreams were born.

Glances of those smiles appears to me in flashes,
it's deep rooted like an ancient banyan viewed in dashes.

Dusted past to paint a picture in memories glow,
Echoes of days from the time we used to know.

Faded dreams bear in mind the twilights cast,
Whispers of a time from the world that didn't last.

Yet through the haze, wind in the heart holds fast,
To lessons learned with difference from the dusted past.

Dusted past, like a music in shadows cast extreme,
Echoes linger every single flash from days long past.

Faded moments creeps within with whispers low,
Traces of a time we want to forget, we used to know.

From the dust of every kind new dreams arise,
Lessons hidden from the scratch in bygone skies.

The phases has treasured memories both of extremes,

Deprivation haunts although few blessings were Supreme.

Dry days made me starve for rains to experience,
Wreath of moods and nature taught to deal with affluence.

"Dusted Past" never went under the wraps falling haywire,
it was, and it will always be in sync with my present like volcanic fire."

44. SILENT WHISPERS

Her startled eyes are narrating the pain
I pray for her, efforts shouldn't go in vain.

I get tantalized by her aura even today,
I pray to be with her all night all day.

I fail to describe her in words or verses,
I pray to heal scars of wounds and bruises.

My peace of mind indulges in her happiness,
I pray to make her genuinely smile for prettiness.

Her eyes are my universe contented to live
I pray for her companionship all life for being alive.

She is my Venus, beauty to the epitome,
I pray for her togetherness with aplomb.

In silent whispers with deep thoughts, hearts align,
A bond forever, that time cannot confine.

Through storm and Sun, we talk as one,
In every step walking miles, our souls entwine.

Hand in hand we face every morning and the night,
In your presence, all feels easy and absolutely right.

Through the life's gifts of highs and all the lows,
Together we breathe, our true strength shows.

Our love is eternal and going to be till last breath,
I pray to Lord, let the purest soul be mine till my death.

45. THE LIES OF MY HEART

"Dripping slowly from ones mouth to brain,
Slipping into the understanding zone without any gain.

Although it gazes, it glares, it freezes, it scares,
My heart displays the emotions for happiness on faces.

Eyes try to speak the untold pain to breathe the breezier,
But "the lies of my heart" are buried which life's expect to feature.

Love is truly a craving that one wish to be blessed with,
unexpected twists and turns shouldn't be the destiny dressed with.

My heart, it speaks in riddled ways, whispers truths that soon betray,
Promises made in fleeting light, fade to shadows by the night sway.

It claims to love, yet knows its art, deceiving even its own heart,
Heart soft and sweet, promises made but never to keep the chart.

White or in black might be our days for reality to ponder,
Irrespective of the moods hold on to emerge much stronger."

46. SUCCESS

Success is considered golden,
By those who have never touched hanger,
To comprehend a challenge,
One requires determined dream and hunger.

Not one of all are the welcoming hosts
Who picked the round to ken today,
telling the correct definition
who is clear of the real victory or success.

Success is born of dreams pursued,
In silent hours, when none intrude.
It rises with each step you take,
A journey made, a future shaped.

With every fall, it learns to grow,
In every challenge, seeds it sow.
Success they say, is not the end,
But in the trials that we transcend.

As I was ruled out…leaving the world
On whose forbidden ear,
The distant strains of victory
exploded terrified, vocal and clear
What success has to say about it!

47. FORGIVENESS

Is always the mightiest sword
Forgiveness of those with the chord.
Is the ever highest reward quants
when they bruise you with taunts?

When they make you feel tiny
Life looks anything but spiny.
When it's hardest to take journey
you may do nothing at all honey.

A heart once happy, burdened with pain,
Finds peace in letting go, the gentle rain.
A bridge rebuilt from words unspoken,
Mends the bonds that once were broken.

In the quiet, a soft embrace,
Forgiveness brings a tender grace.
A healing light where shadows fall,
Love returns and conquers all.

Is the toughest virtue to follow mate,
Forgiveness for those you hesitate.
Is the greatest award in Forde,
when they blame you toward?

When they make you feel small

Just ignore at you every thrown ball.
When it's almost impossible to take knightly
you must do nothing at all honey.

• 80 •

48. RELATIONSHIP CORRELATION (A Sonnet Poem)

In a relationship correlation love is inclined,
Attention is not defined.
Omni presence to obtain,
Understanding and warmth to maintain.

Highest submission to surrender,
In-sync to partners tune don't wander,
Healing each other's agony,
Without colouring emotions in mahogany.

For everything tiny there is no justification,
Feels to touch without giving explanation.
Happiness in any relation shouldn't be measured,
Belongingness is the only thing to be treasured.

Every relationship needs careful nurturing,
Our love for each other kept to ears murmuring.
In love's embrace, loving hearts will always entwine as one,
Though trials may come and shadows may fall, refuge will save the gun.

49. AUTUMN DIARIES

And one fine day the Maple leaf
Was about to take the fall,
The intense wind was rushing
As if being pushed after a stall.

Autumn was here and the leaves
Swayed in no pretence,
The Season of Mists and mystics
Gave blessings in silence.

Stand in the wind and breathe
With each gust to life galore,
Yes, you need to first grab
The canoe and take the oars.

Heat had over brimmed
The effect of not slowing down,
The gushes of the wind
Rhythmical fall of the leave crown.

Autumn's arrival was here to
Check grace of falling leaves,
Pages of the Autumn diaries
Are filled while not to cease.

Sun rises quite high at the

Skyline with ultimate grimace,
falling leaves were on the move
With such beautiful grace.

Be it wind, be it storm wandering
Leaves are to defeat this gust,
When stacked amidst ocean crossing
The water path, is a very must.

50. JEALOUSY

Out of all the feelings,
The deadliest one, which burns us alive,
Ahh! Shall we call it a feeling?
Or a live demon deep inside strive?

This is that ruthless demon
That it's all, adamant not to bend,
and then we blame circumstances
About its reduction to tend.

No! No! It's gnawing hands
Spreads like contemplating's fire,
In spite of trying to take control,
The flames of this grows higher.

Jealousy, without your permission
Barges in the conscious mind,
Ruthless effects thy burning eyes,
Thy dry lips mostly blackened.

Why to envy when each one of us are
Unique and variably different,
It's absolutely impossible to crave and
Imbibe else's contentment.

"Hey Folks!! Let's never

Inadvertently try to torment oneself,
Life is too short way to dwell
In such negativity, save yourself."

51. BE YOU

"Everyone has their own way of perceiving,
Undeterred by others it's an unique achieving.

Encroaching that space should be avoided,
Without judging only character is enjoyed.

"Be You" and let it be to breathe no burden,
Give peace otherwise life will only sadden.

Set your own rules to conquer fearlessly,
Then no looking back to wander aimlessly.

"Be you" in all your presuming windows grace,
A shining light will enlighten life's vast space.

In truth and courage, with every flaw and strength
Find way to embrace your path, its breadth and length.

For in your heart, let doubts and fears not lead astray,
Falling prey to artificiality, please stay always away.

For in our conscience let a fire burns bright,
"Be you" and set the world alight.

Establish courage truly into answer none,

Gather mind for yourself as there's no one.